C000152431

THIS BOOK WILL MAKE YOU FEEL LESS SH*T

summersdale

An Hachette UK Company
www.hachette.co.uk

Summersdale Publishers Ltd
Part of Octopus Publishing Group Limited
Carmelite House
50 Victoria Embankment
LONDON
EC4Y 0DZ
UK

www.summersdale.com

Printed and bound in Croatia

ISBN: 978-1-78685-218-2

Substantial discounts on bulk quantities of Summersdale books are available to corporations, professional associations and other organisations. For details contact general enquiries: telephone: +44 (0) 1243 771107 or email: enquiries@summersdale.com.

TO...........................

FROM......................

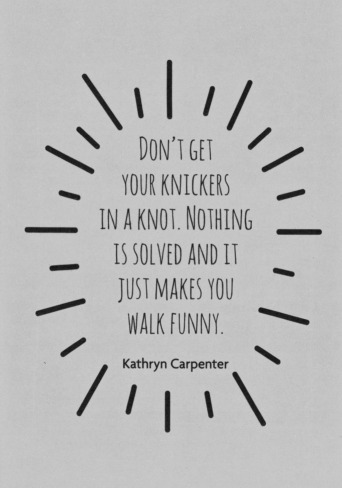

Don't get your knickers in a knot. Nothing is solved and it just makes you walk funny.

Kathryn Carpenter

THIS TIP WILL MAKE YOU FEEL LESS SH*T

GIVE YOURSELF SOMETHING TO LOOK FORWARD TO. EVEN THE SMALLEST TREATS CAN PEP UP YOUR DAY, LIKE PUTTING CRISP, FRESH SHEETS ON YOUR BED OR PREPARING THE INGREDIENTS FOR YOUR DINNER.

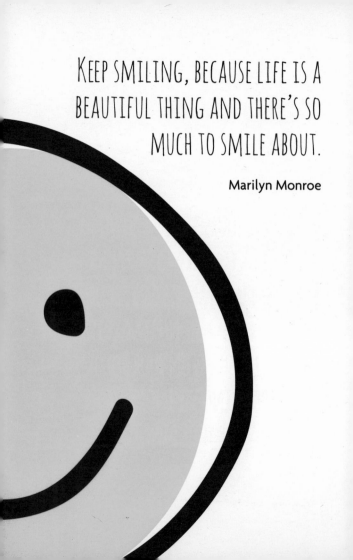

KEEP SMILING, BECAUSE LIFE IS A BEAUTIFUL THING AND THERE'S SO MUCH TO SMILE ABOUT.

Marilyn Monroe

BE OPEN TO
POSSIBILITIES.

THIS TIP WILL MAKE
YOU FEEL LESS SH*T
☺

MAKE A BIG BATCH
OF CHOCOLATE
BROWNIES AND
DON'T FORGET TO
LICK THE BOWL.

EXPECT
PROBLEMS AND
EAT THEM FOR
BREAKFAST.

Alfred A. Montapert

THIS TIP WILL MAKE
YOU FEEL LESS SH*T

MAKE A TO-DO LIST.
THIS HELPS TO RELIEVE STRESS
AND ADD STRUCTURE TO YOUR
DAY — PLUS TICKING EACH
TASK OFF FEELS GREAT.

Those who wish to sing always find a song.

Swedish proverb

THIS TIP WILL MAKE YOU FEEL LESS SH*T

TAKE A BLANKET OUT INTO THE GARDEN, LIE DOWN AND SOAK UP THE SUNSHINE. JUST 10–15 MINUTES OF SUNSHINE A DAY CAN BE ENOUGH TO PROVIDE US WITH SUFFICIENT VITAMIN D.

Focus
on
one
thing
at a time.

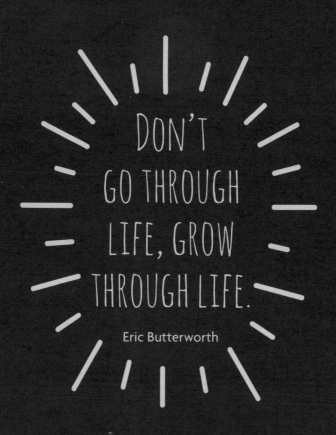

Don't go through life, grow through life.

Eric Butterworth

THIS TIP WILL MAKE
YOU FEEL LESS SH*T

IF IT'S A COLD DAY, BUNDLE UP
WITH THICK BLANKETS AND SIT
OUTSIDE WITH A WARM DRINK.
THE COOLER SEASONS CAN
TEMPT US TO SEEK REFUGE
IN THE WARM INDOORS BUT
FRESH AIR DOES WONDERS
FOR THE SOUL.

CHALLENGE
YOURSELF –
TRY
SOMETHING
NEW.

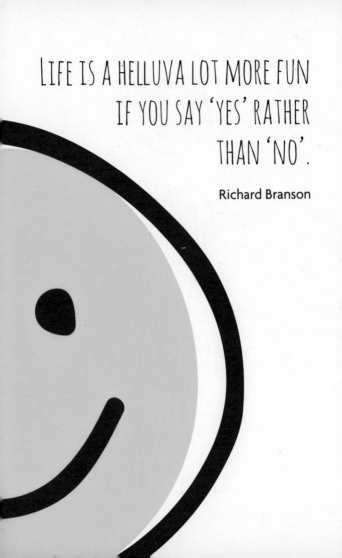

LIFE IS A HELLUVA LOT MORE FUN
IF YOU SAY 'YES' RATHER
THAN 'NO'.

Richard Branson

ACCEPT AND EMBRACE YOUR TRUE SELF.

CURL UP ON THE SOFA AND REREAD YOUR FAVOURITE BOOK FROM YOUR CHILDHOOD — IT'LL BE LIKE VISITING AN OLD FRIEND.

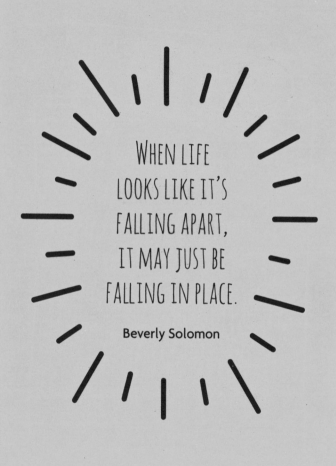

When life looks like it's falling apart, it may just be falling in place.

Beverly Solomon

THIS TIP WILL MAKE YOU FEEL LESS SH*T

Take time away from the computer screen and leave all electronic devices at home. This will relieve the stress of being constantly 'plugged in' and you'll feel calmer and more in touch with the world around you.

BE HAPPY.
IT'S ONE WAY
OF BEING
WISE.

Colette

THIS TIP WILL MAKE YOU FEEL LESS SH*T

WRITE YOUR DREAMS DOWN IN A DREAM JOURNAL AS SOON AS YOU WAKE UP. CREATE A PIECE OF ART, SUCH AS A SHORT STORY OR A DRAWING, BASED ON ONE OF YOUR DREAMS.

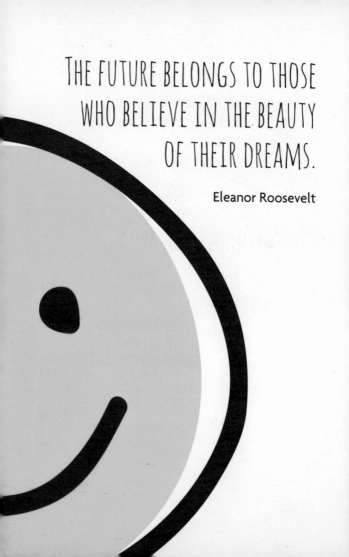

THE FUTURE BELONGS TO THOSE WHO BELIEVE IN THE BEAUTY OF THEIR DREAMS.

Eleanor Roosevelt

DECLUTTER – IT'S
IMPORTANT.
A CLEAN HOME
HELPS TO KEEP
A CLEAR HEAD.

SLOW
DOWN.

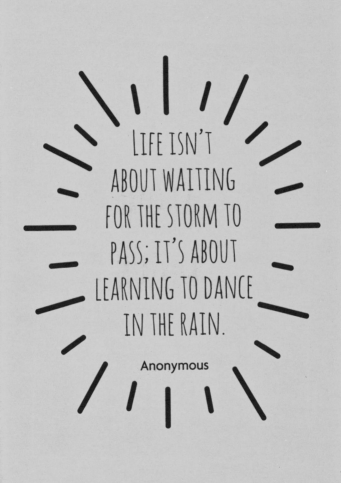

LIFE ISN'T ABOUT WAITING FOR THE STORM TO PASS; IT'S ABOUT LEARNING TO DANCE IN THE RAIN.

Anonymous

THIS TIP WILL MAKE YOU FEEL LESS SH*T

SPEND SOME TIME EVERY DAY
IN THE NEAREST NATURAL SPACE
TO YOU, WHETHER IT'S YOUR
GARDEN, A CITY PARK, THE
RIVERSIDE, THE BEACH OR
THE COUNTRYSIDE.

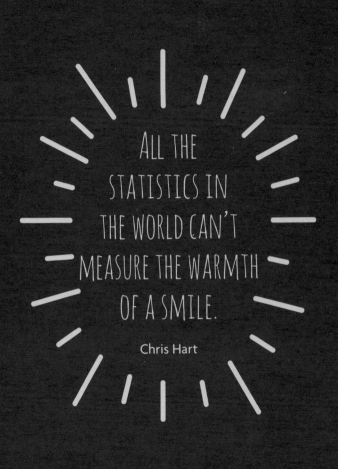

ALL THE STATISTICS IN THE WORLD CAN'T MEASURE THE WARMTH OF A SMILE.

Chris Hart

THIS TIP WILL MAKE YOU FEEL LESS SH*T

IF YOU ARE FEELING STRESSED, TAKE TEN SLOW DEEP BREATHS – YOU'RE GUARANTEED TO FEEL CALMER AFTERWARDS.

TREAT
YOURSELF!

THIS TIP WILL MAKE YOU FEEL LESS SH*T

HAVE A COMFY DAY. PULL ON YOUR OLD AND FAITHFUL OVERSIZED JUMPER, WEAR LOOSE BOTTOMS AND CREATE A LITTLE PILE OF PILLOWS AND BLANKETS TO CURL UP IN. ADD YOUR FAVOURITE BOOK OR PODCAST AND VOILA! THE PERFECT COSY FEELING.

WHY NOT JUST LIVE IN THE MOMENT,
ESPECIALLY IF IT HAS A
GOOD BEAT?

Goldie Hawn

THIS TIP WILL MAKE YOU FEEL LESS SH*T

BUY YOURSELF SOME FRESH FLOWERS TO **BRIGHTEN UP YOUR HOME AND DAY.**

THE SUN
IS NEW
EACH DAY.

Heraclitus

THIS TIP WILL MAKE YOU FEEL LESS SH*T

TALK TO A FRIEND OR YOUR PARTNER WHENEVER YOU FEEL LOW. TROUBLES ALWAYS FEEL SMALLER WHEN THEY ARE SHARED.

Trust
Your
Instincts.

THIS TIP WILL MAKE YOU FEEL LESS SH*T

IF YOU'RE BORED OF MIDWEEK TEA OR SOFT DRINKS BUT YOU WANT TO DODGE THE EFFECTS OF ALCOHOL, TREAT YOURSELF TO A MOCKTAIL.

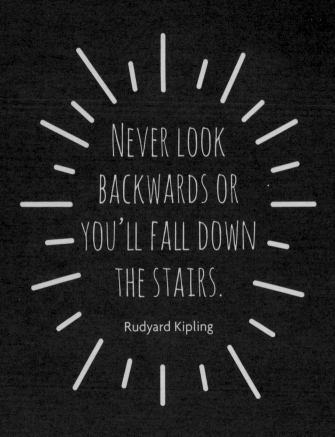

NEVER LOOK BACKWARDS OR YOU'LL FALL DOWN THE STAIRS.

Rudyard Kipling

THIS TIP WILL MAKE YOU FEEL LESS SH*T

KEEP A LITTLE STASH OF FACE MASKS AND OTHER MINI-TREATMENTS TO HAND. THEY ARE A GREAT WAY TO SLIP 20 MINUTES OF SELF-CARE INTO A DAY.

WHEN IT RAINS, LOOK FOR RAINBOWS. WHEN IT'S DARK, LOOK FOR STARS.

IF THINGS ARE GOING UNTOWARDLY ONE MONTH, THEY ARE SURE TO MEND THE NEXT.

Jane Austen

THIS TIP WILL MAKE YOU FEEL LESS SH*T

PUT ON YOUR FAVOURITE TRACK AND ROCK OUT HARD. SING! DANCE! THOROUGHLY ENJOY YOURSELF WITH NO WORRIES THAT SOMEONE MIGHT BE WATCHING.

DO THINGS
THAT
BRING
YOU
JOY.

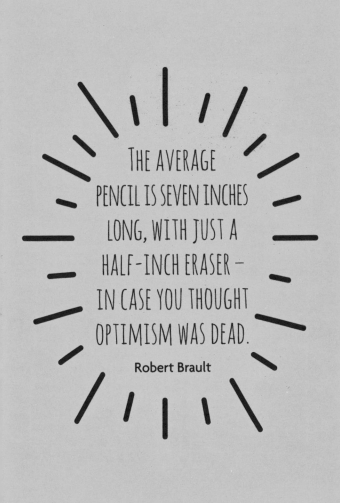

THE AVERAGE
PENCIL IS SEVEN INCHES
LONG, WITH JUST A
HALF-INCH ERASER –
IN CASE YOU THOUGHT
OPTIMISM WAS DEAD.

Robert Brault

LIGHT YOUR FAVOURITE SCENTED CANDLES AND ENJOY AS THEIR FRAGRANCE WAFTS THROUGH YOUR HOME. **It's DIY AROMATHERAPY!**

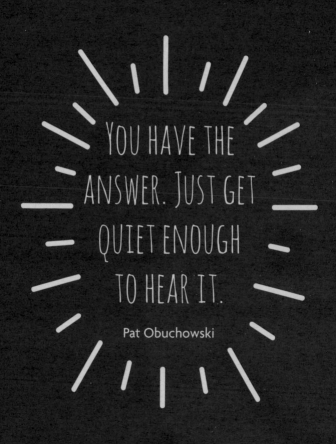

You have the answer. Just get quiet enough to hear it.

Pat Obuchowski

IF THINGS GO WRONG, DON'T GO WITH THEM.

Roger Babson

THIS TIP WILL MAKE YOU FEEL LESS SH*T

IN NEED OF ADVICE?
A GOOD GOSSIP? OR JUST WANT
TO HEAR A FAMILIAR VOICE?
CALL A LOVED ONE.
YOU'LL MAKE THEIR DAY,
AS WELL AS YOURS.

A SMILE IS A FACELIFT THAT'S IN EVERYONE'S PRICE RANGE.

Tom Wilson

THIS TIP WILL MAKE YOU FEEL LESS SH*T

GET INTO THE HABIT OF DRINKING WATER – BEING HYDRATED HELPS TO KEEP YOUR MOOD AND MOTIVATION LEVELS HIGH.

Don't Dehydrate: Rehydrate!

THIS TIP WILL MAKE YOU FEEL LESS SH*T

Think about where you want to be in a year's time and make that first step towards it. This could be as simple as signing up to a new course or going for a quick jog.

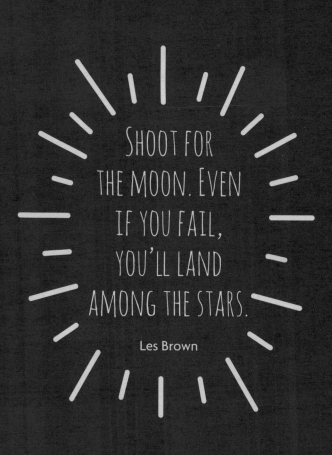

Shoot for the moon. Even if you fail, you'll land among the stars.

Les Brown

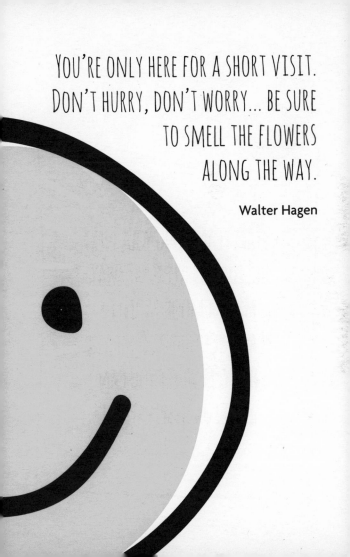

You're only here for a short visit.
Don't hurry, don't worry... Be sure
to smell the flowers
along the way.

Walter Hagen

THIS TIP WILL MAKE
YOU FEEL LESS SH*T

START PLANNING YOUR NEXT
HOLIDAY OR WEEKEND AWAY.
MAKE A MOOD BOARD OF
PLACES YOU WANT TO GO AND
HANG IT WHERE YOU CAN
SEE IT FOR INSPIRATION.

DO ONE THING EVERY DAY THAT SCARES YOU.

Eleanor Roosevelt

THIS TIP WILL MAKE YOU FEEL LESS SH*T

CARRY A PEN AND A LITTLE JOURNAL WITH YOU WHEREVER YOU GO. EVERY TIME YOU FIND YOURSELF AIMLESSLY BROWSING THE INTERNET OR SOCIAL MEDIA ON YOUR PHONE, STOP, AND WRITE A LINE OR TWO ABOUT YOUR DAY IN THE JOURNAL.

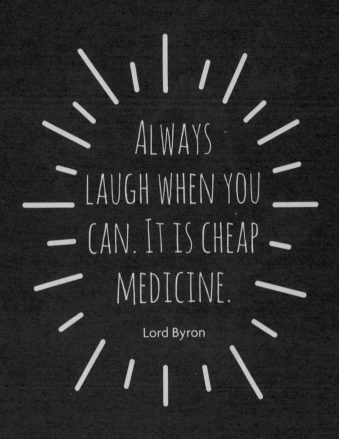

ALWAYS LAUGH WHEN YOU CAN. IT IS CHEAP MEDICINE.

Lord Byron

GOOD FOOD,
GOOD MOOD.

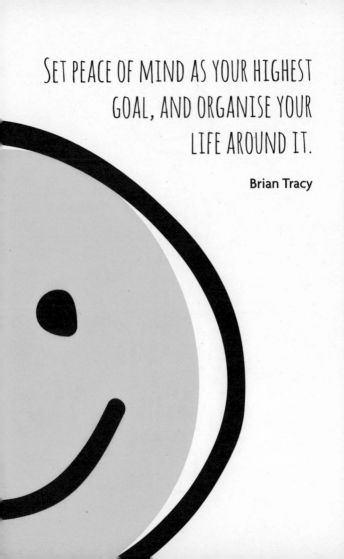

SET PEACE OF MIND AS YOUR HIGHEST
GOAL, AND ORGANISE YOUR
LIFE AROUND IT.

Brian Tracy

FOCUS
ON THE
POSITIVES
IN YOUR
LIFE.

THIS TIP WILL MAKE YOU FEEL LESS SH*T

STOP THINKING 'I'D LOVE TO TRY THAT' AND TURN YOUR DAYDREAMS INTO REALITIES, WHETHER IT'S SIGNING UP TO A NEW CLASS AT YOUR LOCAL GYM OR PAINTING A WATERCOLOUR.

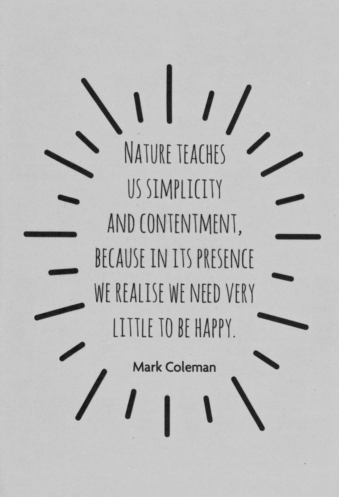

Nature teaches us simplicity and contentment, because in its presence we realise we need very little to be happy.

Mark Coleman

THIS TIP WILL MAKE YOU FEEL LESS SH*T

PLAY YOUR FAVOURITE SONG WHEN YOU GET OUT OF BED IN THE MORNING – IT'S A GREAT START TO THE DAY. CHANGE IT UP EVERY FEW WEEKS TO KEEP THINGS FRESH.

THIS TIP WILL MAKE YOU FEEL LESS SH*T

RUN A NICE WARM BUBBLE BATH AND **WASH THOSE TROUBLES AWAY.**

LET IT GO.

A MULTITUDE
OF SMALL DELIGHTS
CONSTITUTE
HAPPINESS.

Charles Baudelaire

One positive
thought in the
morning can
**CHANGE YOUR
WHOLE DAY.**

THE BEST WAY TO CHEER YOURSELF IS TO TRY TO CHEER SOMEBODY ELSE UP.

Mark Twain

Be yourself,
everyone else
is already
taken.

Oscar Wilde

SAVOUR THE EVERYDAY.

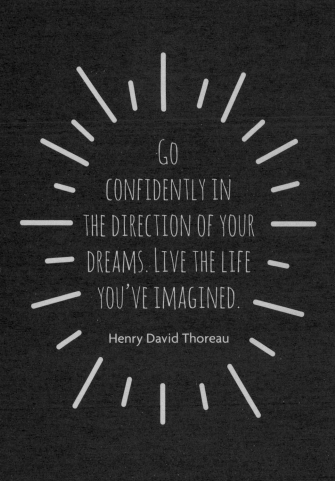

MAKE THIS YOUR MANTRA:
I WILL LOOK AFTER MYSELF TODAY.

BE IN LOVE WITH YOUR LIFE, EVERY DETAIL OF IT.

Jack Kerouac

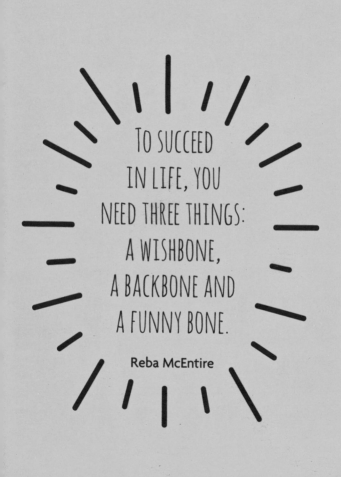

To succeed
in life, you
need three things:
a wishbone,
a backbone and
a funny bone.

Reba McEntire

Do
Something
Today that your
Future Self will
Thank You For.

THIS TIP WILL MAKE YOU FEEL LESS SH*T ☺

TAKE A NAP AND FEEL WELL-RESTED FOR THE REST OF THE DAY.

Chocolate is the answer. Who cares what the question is?!

TOOT YOUR OWN TRUMPET!

THIS TIP WILL MAKE YOU FEEL LESS SH*T

SEARCH ONLINE FOR THE PLANTS AND ANIMALS LOCAL TO YOUR AREA, MAKE A LIST AND THEN GO FOR A WALK. EVERY TIME YOU SPOT ONE TICK IT OFF THE LIST AND PHOTOGRAPH OR SKETCH IT IN YOUR NOTEBOOK.

You are capable of amazing things.

THIS TIP WILL MAKE YOU FEEL LESS SH*T

ORGANISE YOUR WARDROBE TO MAKE YOUR LIFE THAT LITTLE BIT SIMPLER. PERHAPS YOU COULD ARRANGE IT BY COLOUR, GARMENT TYPE OR EVEN OCCASION – THEN YOU'LL ALWAYS FIND IT EASY TO STEP OUT IN STYLE.

DO YOUR
OWN THING.

THIS TIP WILL MAKE YOU FEEL LESS SH*T

GRAB YOUR FAVOURITE MUG AND MAKE **YOURSELF A LOVELY CUPPA.**

Never regret. If it's good, it's wonderful. If it's bad, it's experience.

Eleanor Hibbert

THIS TIP WILL MAKE YOU FEEL LESS SH*T

ROLL OUT YOUR
YOGA MAT.
BREATHE,
MEDITATE,
SIT AND BE STILL.

EVERYTHING
WILL BE OK.

YOU'RE ONLY
YOUNG ONCE,
BUT YOU CAN
BE IMMATURE
FOREVER.

Germaine Greer

THIS TIP WILL MAKE YOU FEEL LESS SH*T

SIT BY A WINDOW IN YOUR HOME WITH YOUR FAVOURITE HOT DRINK AND ENJOY THE VIEW. TRY TO PICK OUT DETAILS OF THE SCENE AND SEE IF YOU CAN SPOT ANYTHING NEW.

I NEVER
LOSE SIGHT OF
THE FACT THAT JUST
BEING IS FUN.

Katharine Hepburn

IF YOU
BELIEVE
IN YOURSELF,
ANYTHING
IS POSSIBLE.

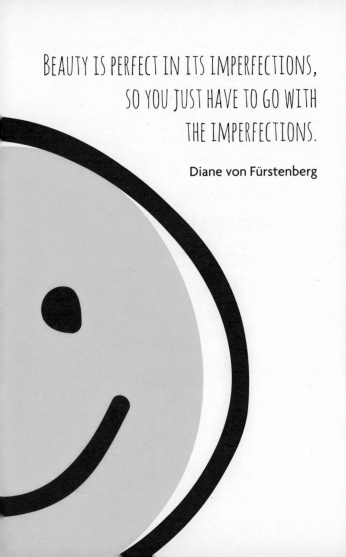

BEAUTY IS PERFECT IN ITS IMPERFECTIONS,
SO YOU JUST HAVE TO GO WITH
THE IMPERFECTIONS.

Diane von Fürstenberg

THIS TIP WILL MAKE YOU FEEL LESS SH*T

WEAR YOUR MOST COLOURFUL OUTFIT TODAY! IF STANDING OUT TOO MUCH GIVES YOU THE CHILLS, START WITH JUST ONE FLASH OF COLOUR. IT WILL LIFT YOUR SPIRITS AND GIVE YOU CONFIDENCE.

Look for the silver linings in life.

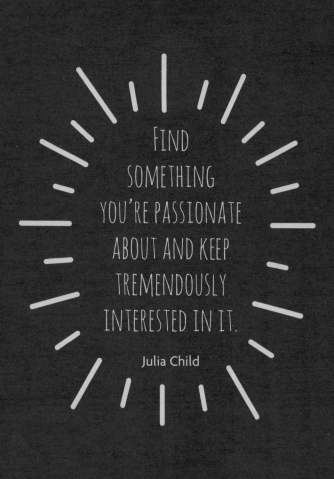

FIND
SOMETHING
YOU'RE PASSIONATE
ABOUT AND KEEP
TREMENDOUSLY
INTERESTED IN IT.

Julia Child

THIS TIP WILL MAKE YOU FEEL LESS SH*T

GATHER SOME ART SUPPLIES, INVITE A GROUP OF FRIENDS AND LOVED ONES TO YOUR HOME, AND SPEND TIME TOGETHER MAKING A MURAL. IT'S A BIT DIFFERENT FROM HAVING PHOTOGRAPHS, BUT EVERY TIME YOU SEE IT, IT WILL REMIND YOU OF THE IMPORTANT PEOPLE IN YOUR LIFE.

LISTEN TO YOUR HEAD, FOLLOW YOUR HEART.

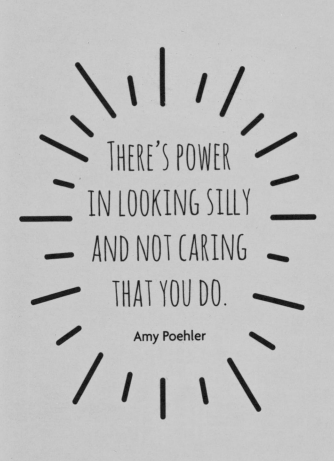

There's power
in looking silly
and not caring
that you do.

Amy Poehler

THIS TIP WILL MAKE YOU FEEL LESS SH*T

CELEBRATE THE RAIN! PULL ON YOUR WELLIES AND FIND SOME PUDDLES TO JUMP IN.

You can break that big plan into small steps and take the first step right away.

Indira Gandhi

THIS TIP WILL MAKE YOU FEEL LESS SH*T

GET RID OF ANY CLOTHING THAT DOESN'T FIT OR FLATTER YOU. IF IT USED TO BE A FAVE GARMENT, BID IT A FOND FAREWELL AND DONATE IT TO A CHARITY SHOP; IT CAN MAKE SOMEONE ELSE AS HAPPY AS IT MADE YOU.

THIS TIP WILL MAKE YOU FEEL LESS SH*T

SMILING RELEASES ENDORPHINS, OUR BODY'S NATURAL FEEL-GOOD DRUG. SO SMILE WHEN YOU CAN!

THIS TIP WILL MAKE YOU FEEL LESS SH*T

DRAW UP A LIST OF ALL THE PLACES YOU WANT TO VISIT LOCALLY AND MAKE PLANS WITH FRIENDS TO GO TOGETHER. THERE ARE SURE TO BE LOTS OF HIDDEN GEMS AROUND YOUR HOME TOWN THAT YOU HAVEN'T BEEN TO YET.

SAY YES TO NEW
OPPORTUNITIES.

LOOK AT EVERYTHING AS THOUGH YOU
WERE SEEING IT EITHER FOR THE
FIRST OR LAST TIME.

Betty Smith

THIS TIP WILL MAKE YOU FEEL LESS SH*T

EAT CAKE – IT'S THE BEST MEDICINE.

There is always something to be grateful for.

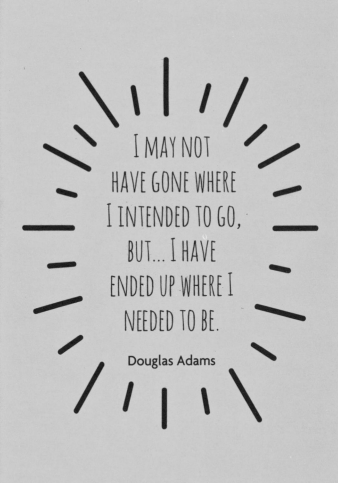

I MAY NOT
HAVE GONE WHERE
I INTENDED TO GO,
BUT... I HAVE
ENDED UP WHERE I
NEEDED TO BE.

Douglas Adams

NEVER
GROW UP.

THIS TIP WILL MAKE YOU FEEL LESS SH*T

PICK AN UPLIFTING QUOTE TO BE YOUR MANTRA FOR THE WEEK. CHANGE THE BACKGROUND OF YOUR COMPUTER SCREEN OR PHONE TO REMIND YOU OF IT.

THINK BIG
THOUGHTS BUT
RELISH SMALL
PLEASURES.

H. Jackson Brown Jr

THIS TIP WILL MAKE YOU FEEL LESS SH*T

REVISIT YOUR CHILDHOOD DREAMS — TRAIN DRIVER, CIRCUS STAR, ICE-CREAM MAKER — AND SEE IF YOU CAN MAKE ONE OF THEM COME TRUE. YOU DON'T HAVE TO BE A PROFESSIONAL, JUST TRY YOUR HAND AT IT FOR THE DAY.

GIGGLING
IS
GOOD
FOR THE
SOUL.

TRY TO BE LIKE THE TURTLE — AT
EASE IN YOUR OWN SHELL.

Bill Copeland

THIS TIP WILL MAKE
YOU FEEL LESS SH*T

STRETCH!
LOOSEN
UP THOSE
MUSCLES.

THIS TIP WILL MAKE YOU FEEL LESS SH*T

CREATE AN EMERGENCY SELF-CARE BOX AND FILL IT WITH THINGS YOU LOVE — YOUR FAVOURITE DVD, A MIXTAPE, TASTY SNACKS. WHEN YOU FIND YOURSELF FEELING BLUE, PICK AN ITEM FROM THE BOX TO HELP LIFT YOUR MOOD.

WHATEVER
IS GOING TO
HAPPEN WILL HAPPEN,
WHETHER WE
WORRY OR NOT.

Ana Monnar

THIS TIP WILL MAKE YOU FEEL LESS SH*T

GET CREATIVE! WHETHER IT'S PAINTING, KNITTING OR WRITING, DEDICATE SOME OF YOUR FREE TIME TO ARTS AND CRAFTS. REMEMBER: THE ACT OF CREATING IS MUCH MORE IMPORTANT THAN ACHIEVING A PARTICULAR SKILL LEVEL.

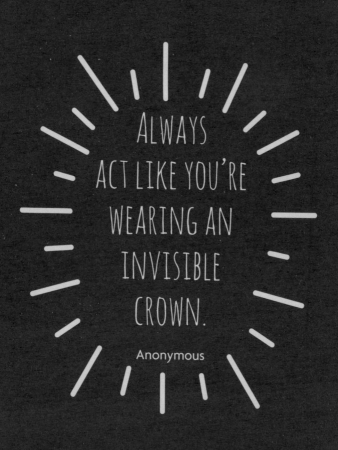

ALWAYS
ACT LIKE YOU'RE
WEARING AN
INVISIBLE
CROWN.

Anonymous

THIS TIP WILL MAKE
YOU FEEL LESS SH*T

WRAP YOURSELF UP WARM
ONE EVENING AND GO TO A
REMOTE, LIGHT-FREE AREA TO
SPEND SOME TIME LOOKING
AT THE TWINKLING STARS. SEE
HOW MANY CONSTELLATIONS
YOU CAN NAME!

My childhood may be over but that doesn't mean playtime is.

Ronald Olson

SHOW THE WORLD WHAT YOU'RE MADE OF!

THIS TIP WILL MAKE YOU FEEL LESS SH*T

SEND A LETTER TO SOMEONE YOU ADMIRE OR WHO INSPIRES YOU. PRAISING OTHERS WILL GIVE YOU A FEEL-GOOD FEELING AND WILL ALSO MAKE THE RECIPIENT FEEL GREAT TOO.

THIS TIP WILL MAKE YOU FEEL LESS SH*T

Go OUTSIDE AND LISTEN TO THE SOUNDS OF NATURE. BE STILL AND ALLOW THE HUMAN SOUNDS, SUCH AS THE HUM OF ENGINES, TO DRIFT PAST YOUR CONSCIOUSNESS, AS YOU TUNE IN TO BIRDSONG AND THE WIND IN THE TREES.

Trust yourself. You know more than you think you do.

Benjamin Spock

THIS TIP WILL MAKE YOU FEEL LESS SH*T

REARRANGE A ROOM IN YOUR HOME. ASK YOURSELF IF THE FURNITURE AND DECORATIONS ARE IN THAT ARRANGEMENT BECAUSE IT'S BEST, OR SIMPLY BECAUSE THEY'VE ALWAYS BEEN LIKE THAT, AND ADJUST YOUR SET-UP ACCORDINGLY.

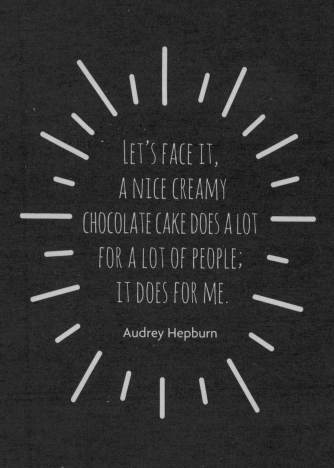

Let's face it,
a nice creamy
chocolate cake does a lot
for a lot of people;
it does for me.

Audrey Hepburn

THIS TIP WILL MAKE YOU FEEL LESS SH*T

TAKE A SMALL AMOUNT OF MONEY TO A CHARITY SHOP AND SEE HOW MANY BOOKS YOU CAN BUY WITH IT. READ ONE THAT AFTERNOON.

Our greatest glory is not in never falling, but in rising every time we fall.

Confucius

THIS TIP WILL MAKE YOU FEEL LESS SH*T

SWAP YOUR NORMAL DINNER FOR A PARTY FOOD PLATTER.

GOOD THINGS
TAKE TIME.

THIS TIP WILL MAKE YOU FEEL LESS SH*T

PHONE A FRIEND AND FIND OUT ALL THEIR NEWS. TOO OFTEN WE ARE FOCUSED ON TALKING AND DELIVERING OUR OWN NEWS, BUT LISTENING IS THE FOUNDATION STONE OF A GOOD FRIENDSHIP.

LIFE IS
MORE FUN
IF YOU PLAY
GAMES.

Roald Dahl

IF LIFE
SEEMS TO BE
TAKING A DETOUR,
ENJOY
THE SCENERY!

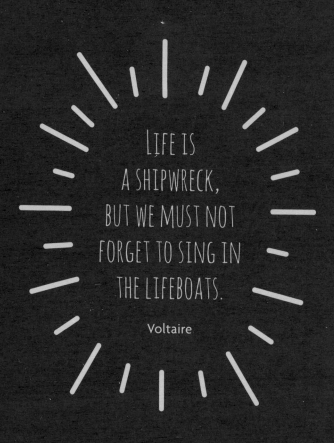

LIFE IS
A SHIPWRECK,
BUT WE MUST NOT
FORGET TO SING IN
THE LIFEBOATS.

Voltaire

THIS TIP WILL MAKE YOU FEEL LESS SH*T

TALK TO SOMEONE NEW. YOU COULD MAKE THEIR DAY – **AND THEY MIGHT MAKE YOURS.**

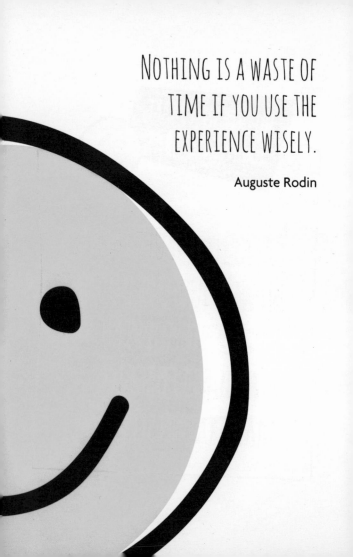

NOTHING IS A WASTE OF
TIME IF YOU USE THE
EXPERIENCE WISELY.

Auguste Rodin

CREATE YOUR ULTIMATE PIZZA – ADD ALL YOUR FAVOURITE TOPPINGS **AND DON'T FORGET THE EXTRA CHEESE!**

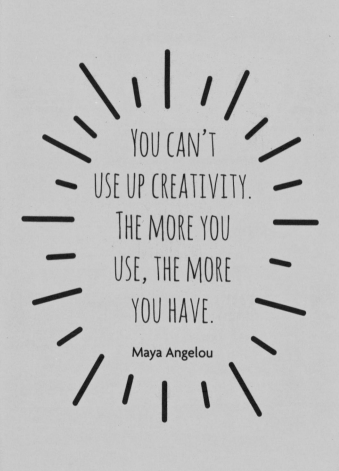

You can't use up creativity. The more you use, the more you have.

Maya Angelou

THIS TIP WILL MAKE YOU FEEL LESS SH*T

KEEP A DAILY JOURNAL TO HELP YOU SEE EACH DAY'S EVENTS MORE CLEARLY. IF YOU CAN'T THINK OF ANYTHING TO SAY, WRITE THE PLACES YOU WENT THAT DAY, ONE THING THAT MADE YOU HAPPY, THE BEST MEAL OF THE DAY AND WHOM YOU SPOKE TO.

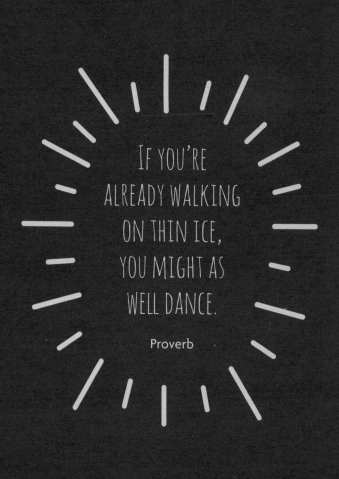

IF YOU'RE
ALREADY WALKING
ON THIN ICE,
YOU MIGHT AS
WELL DANCE.

Proverb

YOU CAN'T TURN BACK THE CLOCK BUT
YOU CAN WIND IT UP AGAIN.

Bonnie Prudden

THIS TIP WILL MAKE YOU FEEL LESS SH*T

WATCH A SAD FILM WITH YOUR BEST FRIEND – **SOMETIMES A GOOD CRY IS JUST WHAT YOU NEED!**

THIS TIP WILL MAKE YOU FEEL LESS SH*T

DOODLE. JUST GRAB SOME PENS AND PAPER, **AND LET YOUR IMAGINATION GO WILD.**

THE BEST
WAY OUT
IS ALWAYS
THROUGH.

Robert Frost

THIS TIP WILL MAKE YOU FEEL LESS SH*T

COOK A NEW RECIPE YOU'VE NEVER TRIED BEFORE. GIVE YOURSELF PLENTY OF TIME TO MAKE IT SO YOU DON'T FEEL ANY PRESSURE, AND RELISH THE FEELING OF LEARNING NEW SKILLS.

HITCH YOUR WAGON TO A STAR.

Ralph Waldo Emerson

THIS TIP WILL MAKE
YOU FEEL LESS SH*T

INVITE FRIENDS OVER,
GET OUT AN OLD BOARD GAME
AND ENJOY TESTING OUT YOUR
LUCK AND SKILL TOGETHER.
JUST TRY NOT TO BECOME
TOO COMPETITIVE!

THIS TIP WILL MAKE YOU FEEL LESS SH*T

SAVE YOUR LOOSE SMALL CHANGE AND ONCE EVERY MONTH OR SO HEAD TO THE ARCADE AND BLOW IT ON THE PENNY MACHINES.

MIX A
LITTLE FOOLISHNESS
WITH YOUR SERIOUS
PLANS. IT IS LOVELY
TO BE SILLY AT THE
RIGHT MOMENT.

Horace

FALL IN LOVE WITH TAKING CARE OF YOURSELF.

Forget past mistakes. Forget failures. Forget everything except what you're going to do now and do it.

William Durant

THIS TIP WILL MAKE YOU FEEL LESS SH*T

MAKE TIME AT THE END OF THE DAY TO WATCH THE SUNSET. PUT AWAY YOUR PHONE AND TURN YOUR FULL ATTENTION TO THE VIBRANT COLOURS OF THE EVENING SKY.

We are all of us stars, and we deserve to twinkle.

Marilyn Monroe

BE GOOD TO
YOURSELF.

If you're interested in finding out more about our books, find us on Facebook at **Summersdale Publishers** and follow us on Twitter at **@Summersdale**.

www.summersdale.com